GET RICH WHILE BLACK ...

Without Being an Athlete, Entertainer or Drug Dealer

GET RICH WHILE BLACK ...

Without Being an Athlete, Entertainer or Drug Dealer

Chuck Starks

Award Winning Entrepreneur

NORCAL BOOKS

Sacramento, California

GET RICH WHILE BLACK

Published by Norcal Books
saclandco@aol.com

Chuck Starks, Publisher & Editorial Director
Yvonne Rose/QualityPress.info, Production Coordinator

Paperback ISBN #: 978-1-7337353-0-8
Ebook ISBN #: 978-1-7337353-2-2
Library of Congress Control Number: 2019902117

DEDICATED TO:

Roslynn

Toby

Ricky

Terron (T.J.)

Jayden

CONTENTS

INTRODUCTION

I Thought That I had it Made (The Good Life)

By the time I was 40 years old, I thought I had it made. I was CEO of my own computer company that I started myself and lived in a beautiful 4-bedroom home with a swimming pool. I had fancy luxury cars and partied every Thursday and Friday at Happy Hour. I took multiple vacations each year to places like the Bahamas, Hawaii, Mexico and Malibu.

Life was fun.

I looked and felt successful. I had reached the American Dream!!!

Then I had a problem with my business partners, and the economy slowed down and I was flat-broke at 45. The home, car, and lifestyle were gone.

I lost my big house that I had purchased when I was 34 years old, which had a huge mortgage payment; the fancy expensive car I drove, which was leased, was repossessed; and I did not have enough savings to sustain myself.

I had maxed out my credit cards, which were used mostly to take my fabulous vacations.

I lost everything and was devastated.

After having worked for myself for over 15 years, I had to find a job. Since I was a well-known computer consultant, I made a few calls and within weeks had a high-paying job as a computer consultant.

Since I was working as an employee, I had plenty of time to think about my situation and plan for the future.

I thought I had done everything right. I got a good education (Computer Programming Certificate from Heald College in Sacramento), worked for a few years in my chosen field (Kaiser Aluminum & Chemical Corporation and others) and started my own business (C E Starks & Associates) on a shoe-string budget with only $200.

By the time I was 40 years old the company I founded had grown to over 45 employees with 5 offices and had clients in multiple states.

And when I had to close my business, I couldn’t believe it. I had been billing millions of dollars a year, and yet I was bankrupt.

What went wrong?

Almost everything. I had to regroup and do things differently. I literally had to change my mindset as to how to be financially successful.

That is what this book is about. The previous ideas that I had, which most people do, were wrong for Black People. I had built my life on credit with no foundation. My clients were primarily governments that were subject to all kinds of factors, most of which were out of my control.

The company I founded provided quality services and won multiple small business awards. I was even "Business of The Year" with our Chamber of Commerce. Even with that, I went out of business – flat broke.

For the next few years, I didn't want to think about going back into business. I gave the few clients that I had left to my partner and decided to work as an employee.

Having been divorced for many years, I remarried at the time I closed my business. I moved into my wife's condominium and tried to be content as an employee, which as an entrepreneur was very difficult for me.

The reason I am writing this book is because of the people I see daily that aspire to make more money and to have a better life. And because I am Black, most of the people I encounter daily are Black.

Many of you live the way I did. You look and maybe feel successful, but you have rented or highly mortgaged homes, buy or lease high-mileage luxury cars, and take vacations each year fueled by credit cards. Some of you even place your children in private schools that you can barely afford.

You live on borrowed money (credit). You have very little or no savings and would not last very long without that check you receive every two weeks or at the end of the month.

Can you imagine the stress that you are under? That stress causes many of the problems in the Black Community.

As you will see in this book, Black Americans have very little real money or assets (net worth), compared to other races, and I will give you information that will allow you to have the kind of life you have only dreamed about. And, without killing yourself by working 80 hours a week or risking all you have to start a business.

After reading this book you will be able to develop a proven plan to gain more financial wealth, more time to spend with your family, and a much more secure future.

Whether you are young or old, white-collar, blue-collar, or no-collar, you will be able to be financially successful.

The concepts discussed in this book will work for anyone with an income. Even if you are a professional athlete or entertainer this book will allow you to secure your future sooner, because your income is much higher than normal.

I have read that 65% of professional athletes are bankrupt within 5 years of retirement and most entertainers might have a hit or two; but as they get older their earning power greatly diminishes, yet they try to maintain the same usually extravagant lifestyle.

And if you are a drug dealer – QUIT TODAY - and get a job, otherwise you will end up dead or in jail. You don't have to commit crimes to get rich. Just follow the concepts of this book.

You will have control of your success and no one, Black, White or otherwise will be able to stop you from reaching your financial goals.

This is not a get-rich-quick book where you can get rich overnight. I do not discuss multi-level marketing schemes or borderline legal opportunities.

I will discuss a proven overtime way that anyone in this great Country of ours, Black or White, can become rich now and create wealth for their heirs in the future.

I purposely did not include information about my personal politics or religion because I did not want to give anyone an excuse for not using this strategy and getting rich.

I have been extremely successful in life, partly due to the fact that I was raised by Black parents in a White neighborhood with daily contact to White People. I consider myself intellectually Bi-Racial (IBR), which means I can act and think like Black and White People, simultaneously.

As a child, I considered it a curse to be IBR; but as I grew, I found out that knowing what people were thinking and what they expected of me added greatly to my success.

Also, I had no inferiority complex that many Blacks have when dealing with Whites, since I interacted with White people daily. I knew early on that White people were not inherently smarter than Black People and that they were not to be feared or overly respected.

I always knew that I was Black, but I never considered myself inferior to anyone.

I was not really accepted by Black People or White People. I was clearly Black, but I sounded and acted White. This was not an act and was my normal self. I simply acted like the people who were around me, which were mostly White.

I also had a thing for living well and always had a nice home and nice cars with plenty of money, and Black and White People seemed confused as to how I could live that way.

So, I didn't fit in and was viewed with suspicion.

I will speak more about this in the second part of this book.

This book is for anyone who desires to be financially successful, and especially for Black People because of our unique experiences with racial discrimination in America.

As you will see, Black People are, per capita, poorer than most other Americans.

I have broken this book down into two parts. The first part is about the current plight of Black People in America with a proven strategy to get rich.

This strategy will work for anyone, whether you are self-employed, work for the Government, are a teacher, police officer, lawyer, doctor, carpenter, plumber, barber, janitor, electrician, auto repair person, or secretary. If you have an income, you can become financially successful.

If you work on a job, you can, by following this strategy, become a millionaire in America, and you can start at any age.

The second part of the book is about myself and my career and how I came to my conclusions.

PART 1

WHY ARE BLACK AMERICANS POOR?

I BELIEVE BLACK PEOPLE IN AMERICA ARE POOR BY DESIGN OF THE AMERICAN SYSTEM. The plan was to enslave Black People and once/if they are freed, to make them perpetual second-class-citizens that would be relegated to menial jobs, substandard living, ill health, poverty and early death. This is how some 3rd World Countries treat their perpetually underclass people and many are called "untouchables".

SLAVERY, JIM CROW, RACISM, DISCRIMINATION

Laws (Jim Crow) that supported racial discrimination gave Whites access to more and better goods and services and were designed to mentally keep Blacks down by making them see and feel that they were less than Whites and were of a lower-class. This was done by posting 'White and Black Only' signs in public places and not allowing Blacks access to many hotels and restaurants or quality housing.

- Statistics – Pew Research Center Report (2013) – Black Americans have an average net worth of $11,000 – White Americans have an average net worth of $141,900. 1 in 7 White families have a net worth over $1 Million Dollars. 1 in 50 Black families have a net worth over $1 Million Dollars.
- Asian Americans have an average net worth of $89,300 and Hispanic Americans have an average net worth of $13,700.

Note: Net worth refers to the value of items owned, including: real estate, cars, checking and savings accounts, and stocks/bonds with debt (liabilities) subtracted.

This disparity in net worth creates a feeling in Blacks that they are not as good, or as smart as Whites. Whites, due to their ability to inherit property for the 300 years of slavery and beyond, during Jim Crow, maintain a much better lifestyle and overall quality of life than Blacks with much more money to spend (disposable Income).

Blacks see Whites live in better neighborhoods, drive better cars, go to better schools and have much more money to spend, which causes them to have a much-lower opinion of themselves, feeling that they are not as smart or hard-working as Whites. This inferiority complex in many Blacks was the goal of their mistreatment by Whites during slavery and the Jim Crow years.

Oftentimes the excuse given by Blacks and Whites as to the poverty of Blacks, is that Blacks do not work together, or as hard. That is not true. Blacks in America are poor due to racial discrimination – short and simple.

WHAT IS BEING RICH IN AMERICA?

- Having more than enough money to take care of your family and live well.
- Acquiring a net worth of over $1 Million Dollars that will afford you a good life now and the ability to leave a good inheritance to your heirs.

NOTES:

____

____

____

____

____

____

____

____

____

____

____

____

WHY ARE OTHER MINORITIES IN AMERICA PROSPERING?

- Many minorities from other Countries have a connection to their home country and spend money among themselves almost exclusively when they get here. There are people from their place of origin that can provide them with money that helps them survive as well as start and maintain businesses in this Country.
- Whites vilify Blacks more than any other minority group, due to their connection to the depravity of slavery. Many Whites justify their discrimination of Blacks as a validation of slavery

NOTES:

____

____

____

____

____

____

HOW CAN BLACK AMERICANS PROSPER IN AMERICA?

- Stay out of jail – Do not commit crimes.
- Get as much education as possible – BA/BS Degree or above preferred - so you can get a good high-paying job.
- Invest in Real Estate as soon as possible and continue to acquire property during your lifetime for additional rent income and to provide ample inheritance to your heirs.
- If you want your own business, don't start a business from scratch – buy a franchise.

Whether you are a barber, salesman, fireman, executive, Government Employee, policeman, doctor, lawyer, teacher, etc., you can become rich if you do what is contained in this book.

When Blacks start a business, they are basically alone with a possible good idea for a product or service, but with no backup financial resources when you need them, most fail within the first year.

NOTES:

BLACK-OWNED BUSINESSES IN AMERICA (PEW REPORT)

Black-owned businesses in the United States **increased 34.5%** between 2007 and 2012 totaling **2.6 million Black firms**. More than 95% of these businesses are mostly sole proprietorship or partnerships which have no paid employees. About **4 in 10 black-owned businesses** (1.1 Million) in 2012 operated in the health care, social assistance; and other services such as repair, maintenance, personal and laundry services sectors.

As you see from the following chart, Black Businesses make much less money than other businesses in America, with most Black Businesses operated by the owner with no employees. These businesses barely support the owner and have very little chance of long term success, or being passed on to heirs.

The Power of Business Ownership

BlackDemographics.com

White-owned businesses	Asian-owned businesses	Hispanic-owned businesses	Black-owned businesses
Create 55.9 million jobs*	Create 3.8 million jobs	Create 2.5 million jobs	Create 1 million jobs
which is enough to	which is enough to	which is enough to	which is enough to
employ 44% of the working-age White population	employ 33% of the working-age Asian population	employ 8% of the working-age Hispanic population	employ 4% of the working-age Black population
and with annual revenues of	and with annual revenues of	and with annual revenues of	and with annual revenues of
$12.9 Trillion	$793.5 billion	$473.6 billion	$187.6 billion
they could give EVERY working-age White American a check for	they could give EVERY working-age Asian American a check for	they could give EVERY working-age Hispanic American a check for	they could give EVERY working-age Black American a check for
$102,000	$67,000	$14,000	$7,000
EVERY YEAR	EVERY YEAR	EVERY YEAR	EVERY YEAR

*Jobs = hired employees. This does not include owners of businesses who only employ themselves.
Source: U.S. Census Bureau, 2012 Survey of Business Owners, 2012 Census Bureau Annual Estimates of the Resident Population by Sex, Single Year of Age, Race, and Hispanic Origin for the United States: Population Division
Black-owned business: Blacks or African Americans own 51 percent or more of the equity, interest, or stock of the business.
Working-age adults ages 18-64. All figures are rounded. Created by BlackDemographics.com

Black Demographics.com

Due to slavery, Blacks lost their connection to any Country; and thus, are not able to receive financial assistance or support for their businesses from their country of origin, when necessary, as other minority groups.

Business Education (Business 101) states that before you start a business you should borrow money from your family and friends and go to a bank for a loan. Our problem is that most, if not all, of our family and friends are Black with an average net worth of $11,000 compared to the average net worth of Whites - $141,900 (Pew Research Center Report – 2013). Most Blacks barely have enough money to live on, let alone money to invest or the ability to get a business loan.

WHY BLACK BUSINESSES FAIL

It is clear that Black Americans are not successful in business, simply because they do not have the education or experience. They do. Blacks have the experience with degrees from some of the best colleges in the country and having been top executives and CEOs of some of the largest and best-run companies in America (even President of the United States).

Some Blacks have enough money to start a business, but when there is financial crisis, and in all businesses there will be a financial crisis, they fold. But why, since Black people have been living and working in this country for centuries, do they have less and make less? The difference, we all know, is that Black people were working as unpaid slaves for hundreds of years and during those years they were not only not being paid, but they were not creating assets or net worth of their own that they could pass down to their offspring (inheritance).

Most rich Whites in America are wealthy due to inheritance.

If each Black family was given 40 acres and a mule as promised in 1865, its value would be worth approximately $1.6 million dollars today in land value alone (not counting the mule). Black people would be in a much better situation financially today, if the promise had been kept. But that never happened.

Being in a White business is like being on the ocean in a boat. Large or small boat, it does not matter. Being in a Black business is like being in the ocean without a boat (swimming in the water), meaning you have impending danger from all sides - of being eaten by sharks and/or other fish, being run over by the boats of other businesses – or just getting tired and sinking to the bottom. And, you have to figure out a way to feed yourself and your family, while you are treading water and dealing with sharks, boats and the elements.

The stress of running a small business has killed more than one Black person with a great idea and excellent entrepreneurial skills.

But, some Black people do start businesses and usually struggle for many years, with the owner the only employee or the owner working a second job to maintain their dream (business), then they go out of business due to a multitude of reasons (sickness, fatigue, lack of business/money or competition - fair and otherwise) and conversely do not pass assets to their offspring which means their progeny must start the process all over again from scratch, with no assets.

And most children of Black business owners do not want to take over the family business because they saw with their own eyes, first-hand, the struggles of running a Black business; long hours, fatigue, lack of money, lack of family time, etc.

DON'T START A BUSINESS ACQUIRE A FRANCHISE

By acquiring a franchise, possibly by refinancing real estate, you will be able to create the resources and support necessary to be successful. I can assure you that whatever you want to do, there is an available franchise.

As an example, the most successful group of Black Businesses in America are the National Black McDonald's Operators Association. There are about 350 members with an average net worth of approximately $7.5 Million (yes … millions).

By acquiring a franchise (franchisee) you are creating a support system, similar to what other minority groups that have a connection to their country of origin. By having a strong financial backer (franchisor) you are not alone and if anyone comes at you, they have to deal with your big brother (franchisor).

YOU MUST INVEST IN REAL ESTATE - HOW DO YOU GET STARTED?

Some of the wealthiest people in America, own real estate. Because Whites have been acquiring and inheriting property for the 300 years while Blacks were slaves, many Blacks do not own property to live in or to pass down to their family.

During Jim Crow, Blacks, if they could buy land, the land was in the worst parts of town, which appreciated the least.

Now there is no reason for Blacks not to buy property in any part of town and by developing a plan, Blacks can become rich with little concern for how Whites or others feel about them.

As a rental property owner (landlord) myself, I can tell you that potential tenants do not care about the race of the landlord, only that they provide a safe place to live.

Almost 40% of people in this country pay rent each month for their home or apartment. By acquiring a number of small multifamily residential properties, while you are working, you can increase your monthly income and net worth substantially.

I call these types of investors, "Mom and Pop" investors.

Making investments in multifamily real estate allows for maximum control of your investment and also provides for an increasing income stream, now, and if managed correctly, a very robust retirement in the future.

And, your chances of losing your entire real estate investment are relatively low, compared to some stocks and other investment vehicles.

When you purchase your first home, buy a duplex. Live in one side and rent out the other. This will allow you to have multiple income streams. Income from your job, your spouse's job if you are married, and the income from the other duplex unit.

In a few years, you can acquire another rental property, maybe by refinancing the first, and have even more income at the end of each month.

When your income reaches an acceptable level, you can buy your first "dream home" with the income from your job(s) and rental income.

I cannot recommend investing in stocks and bonds. I don't understand how it works, and based on the comments I hear from stock brokers, they don't know either.

In my opinion, Mom and Pop Real Estate Investors are a husband and wife or small group of investors that own and manage less than 20 rental housing units, while working full-time jobs (some or all). The rental income supplements their wages from the jobs, which allows them to maintain a better and more secure lifestyle. The income these investments produce is normally $800 to $20,000 per month (for about 20 or less units).

Real Estate Investors make money 3 ways: (1) rent income, (2) property appreciation, and (3) tax write-offs (depreciation).

The investment strategy (goal) should be to acquire income properties to hold until their mortgages are paid off, allowing for ample income in retirement and a hefty inheritance to heirs.

When determining whether to buy an income investment property, location is the most important factor. The location of the property should be safe and in an up and coming area –

meaning an area that was possibly depressed at one time, but is now improving. Buying property in upscale areas is a strategy, if you can find them, but you will normally pay a premium, with not much upside (cash flow) potential, without a major down payment.

The down payment should be the lowest amount possible that still allows the property to produce cash each month. Low down payments allow for maximum return-on-investment (ROI).

Some lenders are now offering 5% down payment loans on duplexes and 10% down loans on fourplexes. For larger apartments, a 25 – 35% down payment is normally required.

It is important to look for properties that require some improvements, and with those improvements (made by you) the property should cash flow (produce clear income) within months from acquisition. The cash flow only has to be a few dollars each month after the mortgage payment, plus expenses (taxes, insurance, basic maintenance).

Look for properties that are in an improving area, and have a good foundation/structure, good plumbing and good electrical. Other factors, such as minor structural damage (walls, ceilings, floors) is no major concern. A good handyman or contractor can repair minor structural concerns without major cost. Counter tops, carpet and tile will normally have to be replaced, as well as interior painting and exterior cosmetic touchup. The cost to "totally" renovate each unit is around $2,500 and should last from 5 – 10 years with normal use.

The identified property should not need a complete exterior painting or a new roof. If it does, those costs should be deducted from the listing price, before your offer is made.

When the days-on-the-market (DOM) is less than 30, the best offer is a full-price offer; or if the property is extremely desirable, I would suggest an offer a little over list price. If the DOM is greater than 30, and it is considered a good deal by your cash flow projections (income estimates) you should offer less than full-price. The seller will normally counter your offer with the amount that is needed to do the deal or they might accept your offer. If the countered amount is higher than your cash projection permits, you might want to pass on the property or come up with a better way to structure the purchase.

At no time should you purchase income property that will not cash flow within a few months, unless you have other compelling reasons. Properties that do not cash flow are negative assets and, in my opinion, should be avoided.

If you are interested in a property, the first thing you should do is drive by the property during the day and night, including 3 or 4 blocks around the property, then decide if you want to invest in the area.

If you want to pursue the property after you have driven the area, the property background should be researched, and a cash flow projection should be developed by your real estate agent (agent).

If the cash flow projection meets your requirements, an offer should be developed, based on the identified financial components (mortgage, area rents, etc.) and submitted by your agent.

In order to make an acceptable offer, you will normally need a deposit check for 1% of the offered price and a pre-qualification letter from your lender or bank for the amount of the offer.

Once an offer is accepted, which could be after numerous counteroffers, the process to purchase normally takes from 30 – 60 days, depending on contingencies (things that must be done before the close).

Remember - you have an inspection period to completely inspect the property and if concerns are noted, you can modify the offer or pass on the deal (cancel the offer).

It is very important to work with a real estate agent that is an experienced investor and is knowledgeable about income property management.

When you are ready to rent out your property, place a sign in the yard and place an ad in your local paper or rental website. There are housing programs that assist you find renters such as Section 8, Homeless Veterans Program and others that have people looking for housing and have Websites where you can list your property.

Always screen your potential tenants well. I always run a credit check and contact their prior landlord as to the type of tenant they are. If they have a prior eviction, be very careful when renting to them.

Before you make your first investment property purchase, I would suggest you join your local Rental Housing Association. The services and information provided by these associations are invaluable to new as well as experienced real estate investors.

PART 2

CHUCK'S CAREER AND LIFE EXPERIENCES

I was born in Fresno, California and moved to Sacramento when I was 1 month old in 1951. My father bought a new car in 1951, a month after I was born, and wanted to show the car and me to his mother in Texas. After spending time in Texas on the way back to Fresno, my family stopped by my dad's cousin's house in Sacramento. While there my father heard that they were hiring construction workers to build Folsom Dam.

My father applied and got a job building the dam.

My father and mother moved all of our belongs to Sacramento. We never moved back to Fresno.

My parents were strong Black People and preached honesty and did not have a racist bone in their body.

I have 3 brothers (2 are deceased) and 2 sisters.

My older brother was a star football player and my sister was elected Home-coming Queen, at our almost all-White high school.

When I was 4 years old my family moved to Rio Linda, California which was a farming community outside of Sacramento.

Rio Linda was almost all-White with only a few Black Families.

I had a normal childhood and even had a horse. Not that the family had horses, I had my own horses that I bought with my own money. Since we lived on a large lot in the country, my father and I built a fenced yard and barn.

I have worked since I was 8 years old. First cleaning stalls at a horse ranch, then having 2 paper routes, morning and evening. I washed dishes in restaurants while in high school, and worked behind the counter of a liquor store and played music in bands while in college.

I have always liked making money and I seemed to always have more money than my brothers and sisters.

I went to school in Rio Linda graduating in 1969. We had White People in our house every day, from my mother's friends, my school friends, my sister's friends, to my brother's best friend who was always getting kicked out of his house.

I never had any major racial problems. Or, maybe I just didn't notice. There were people that didn't like me; but I never thought it was because I was Black. I thought it was for other reasons, which I'm sure was very naïve.

We had gangs or groups; but there were Black, White and Hispanics on both sides. There was an Asian guy who went both ways, depending on the situation.

No major problems. Just a few fistfights occasionally and then we would all hang out together at the Archway, later that evening. You might have heard of the famous Archway, which was a hamburger stand that President Bill Clinton loved to frequent because he loved their food.

From the time I was about 13 years old, I was a musician and played in many bands.

After high school my father asked me what I was going to do. I told him I was going to be a rock star with my band and make a lot of money like the Jackson 5, James Brown and the Fabulous Flames, and others.

He asked me what I would do if the band did not make it. I hadn't though of that. I told him I didn't know. One day while watching TV, I saw a commercial with a nicely dressed guy with a beautiful girl, getting out of a convertible, saying that he was a computer programmer and how his life was great. I don't remember the school he was promoting, but that afternoon I looked in the phone book for computer schools and eventually went to Heald Business College and received a Computer Programming Certificate two years later.

Soon after, I got a job as a computer operator/programmer and stayed in the computer business for the next 30 years.

I got married in 1971.

After various computer programming jobs, I started my own computer consulting/programming company, C E Starks & Associates, in 1980, on my 29th birthday (May 14th).

After some lean years, I changed the name to ComputerTech Integrators, Inc., and became an IBM Business Partner (computer franchisee), selling and supporting IBM PC's and Mini-Computers.

The business grew rapidly and in 1989 was awarded the INC. 500 Award for being one of America's Fastest Growing Companies. In 1991 the company won multiple IBM Top Gun Awards for sales and quality service. Our company was ranked number one (#1) in our 11-state region.

Within 2 years my relationship with IBM soured and they canceled my contracts for no valid reason. I sued them for breach of contract and won a 6-figure settlement.

Without the IBM Business Partnership (franchise), the company failed.

Even though I had sales of over $5 Million in some years, I was financially broke in 1997 and eventually lost the home I had purchased in 1985.

Since I was a well-known computer expert and consultant, I went to work for various companies and in 1998 me and my wife purchased our first rental property, a 2-unit duplex that was in very bad shape.

Actually, it was my wife Roslynn's idea to purchase rental property. Like most people, I dreaded having to deal with tenants and the concerns of being a landlord. But since my wife had experience with rentals, because her uncle was a landlord, she convinced me to give it a try. And I am glad she did. I actually love being a landlord and owning rental property.

After renovating the duplex and placing tenants, we purchased other rental properties and our current home (yes – 4 bedrooms with a swimming pool) within the next few years.

Our net worth went from zero to over $1 Million Dollars within a few years by buying and renovating rental property, while both me and my wife were working.

We manage our own property and in 2001, I received my real estate license, and have been selling commercial real estate (apartments) since 2008.

We currently have more than a million-dollar net worth and own and manage multiple rental properties in Sacramento, California.

SUMMATION

1. Remember, you are not inferior to anyone. If you are Black and poor, it is by design of this system and you must work diligently to free your mind of the shackles of an inferiority complex.

2. Do not commit crimes to try to get rich – you will end up dead or in jail.

3. Get as much education as you can (Bachelor's Degree preferred) so you can make as much money as possible on your job.

4. Stay on your job and buy as much income producing real estate as possible, as soon as you can. It doesn't matter what kind of job you have, as long as you have enough income to buy real estate. You can refinance the real estate if you decide to become self-employed.

5. If you want to own your own business, buy a franchise so you will have the financial support (backup) of a major corporation to help you start and stay in business.

6. Also, one other thing that I think is important; give a portion of your income to a charity, your Church or

directly to the poor. Giving creates a feeling in you that you have more than enough. Whether you actually have more than enough or not, you do have enough to give and help other people. I personally have been giving 10% of my income to my Church for many years, even in down times.

If you follow the strategies addressed in this book you will be much stronger financially and possibly get rich within a few years. If you decide to go into business, hopefully with a franchise, continue to buy real estate to bolster your net worth.

Don't Hate

You don't have to hate or try to keep anyone down to get rich in America. The advantage that Whites have (White Privilege) was created long ago and most Whites do not hate Blacks and conversely most Blacks do not hate Whites. Yes, there seems to be a nervousness between the races, and maybe a lack of trust, but hating or even disliking a whole race of people is counter-productive and is just plain stupid and a waste of time.

Just do what is in this document and you and your family will be able to live the way you want to live with much more money, and you might possibly get rich.

And remember,
you are not inferior to anyone.

CHUCK'S ACHIEVEMENTS

Board of Director Participation

- State of California Small Business Development Board (California Senate Appointment)
- University of California Davis Medical Center Community Advisory Board (Chairman)
- University of California Davis Student Outreach Board
- American River College Advisory Board
- Sacramento Black Chamber of Commerce Board (Co-Founder)
- Sacramento County Education Skills Center Board

Business Accomplishments/Awards

- NAACP - Outstanding and Dedicated Service Award (1987)
- INC. Magazine 500 Fastest Growing Business Award (1989)
- Malcolm Baldrige National Quality Award (1990)
- Sacramento Black Chamber of Commerce - Business of The Year (1990)
- IBM Top Gun Sales and Service Awards (2-1991)

- Sacramento Observer Newspaper – Northern California Outstanding Black Business Award (1991)
- Sacramento Business Journal – One of Sacramento's Largest Certified Minority Owned Businesses Award (1992)
- United States of America Department of Commerce – Retail Firm of the Year Award (1992)

ABOUT THE AUTHOR

Chuck Starks is a Black American raised in Rio Linda, a rural area outside of Sacramento, California. He was in the computer business for over 30 years and started investing in income real estate in 1998.

He received his real estate license in 2001 and is a real estate investor and commercial agent living in Sacramento and has no plans to retire.

He is married and has 2 daughters and 3 grandchildren (two boys and a girl).

YOU HAVE

MY PERMISSION

TO GET RICH!!!

NOTES:

NOTES:

NOTES:

NOTES:

NOTES:

www.ingramcontent.com/pod-product-compliance
Lightning Source LLC
Chambersburg PA
CBHW071518210326
41597CB00018B/2803

* 9 7 8 1 7 3 3 7 3 5 3 0 8 *